Woof Woo

NAME :

BIRTHDAY :

FAVORITE FOOD :

FAVOURITE PLACE :

Paw print

Henlo. I am ....

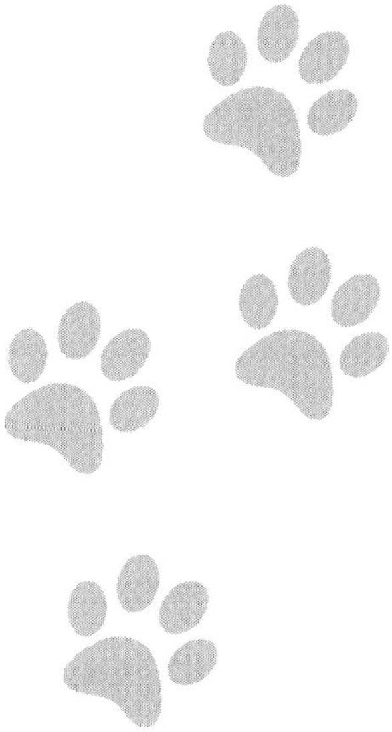

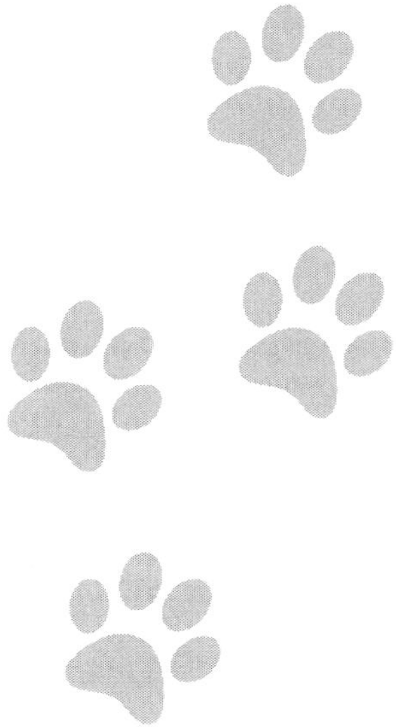

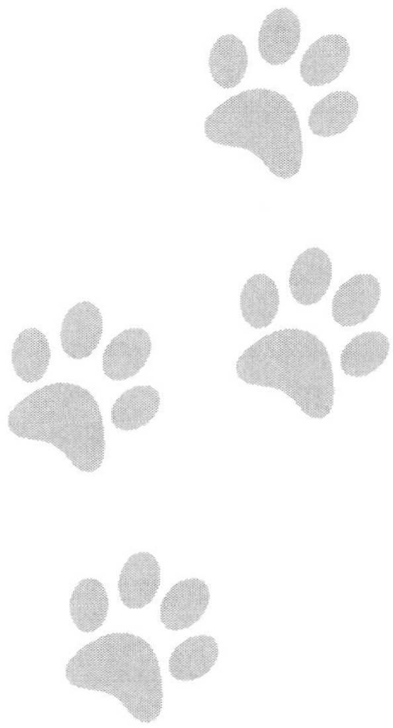

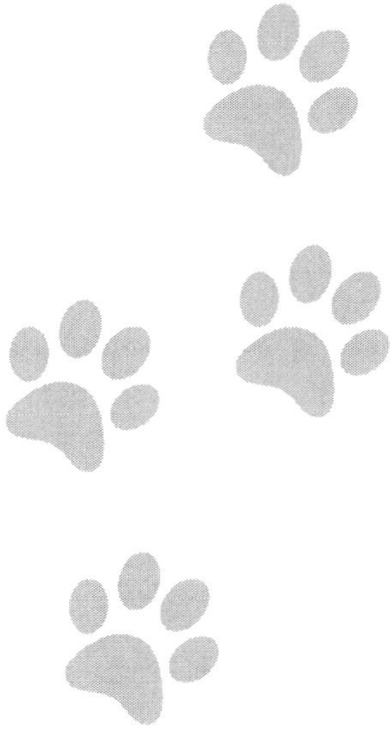

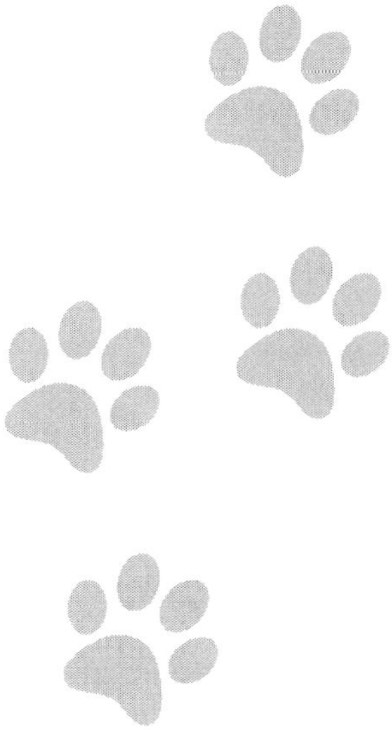

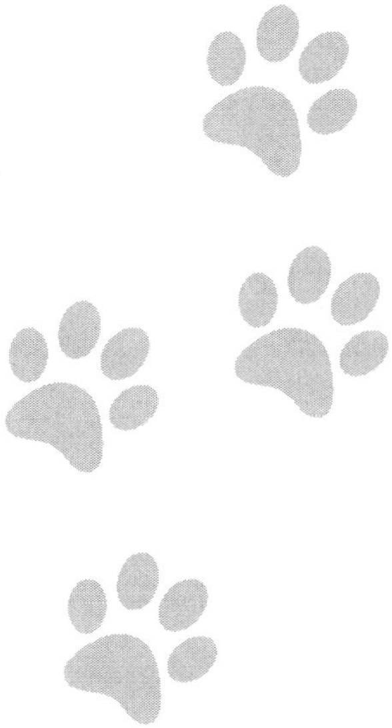

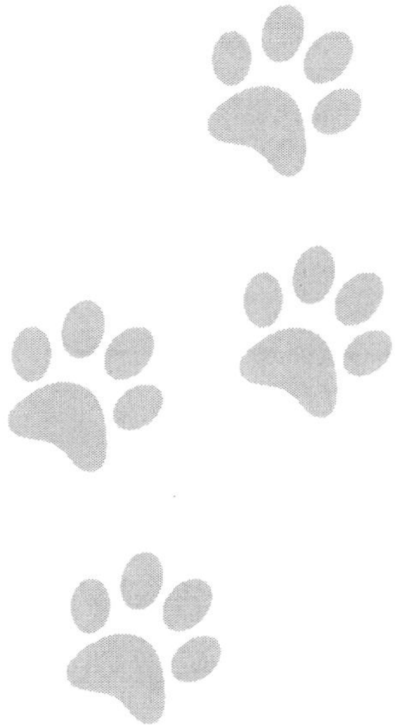

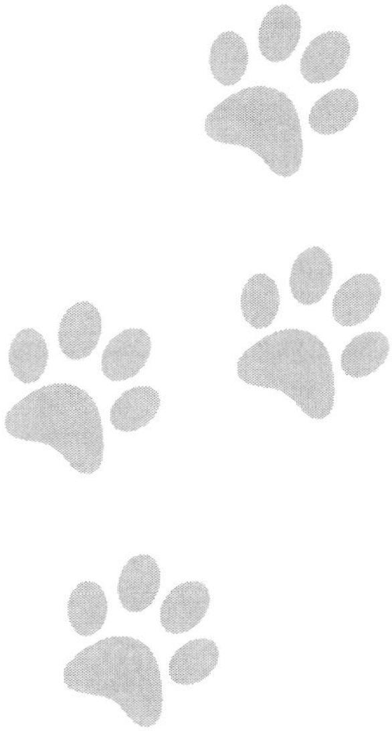

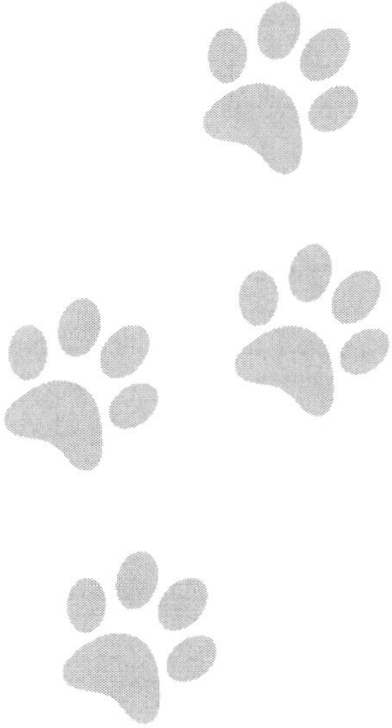

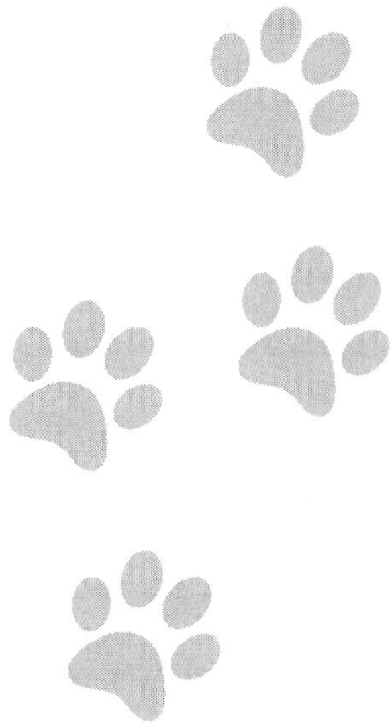

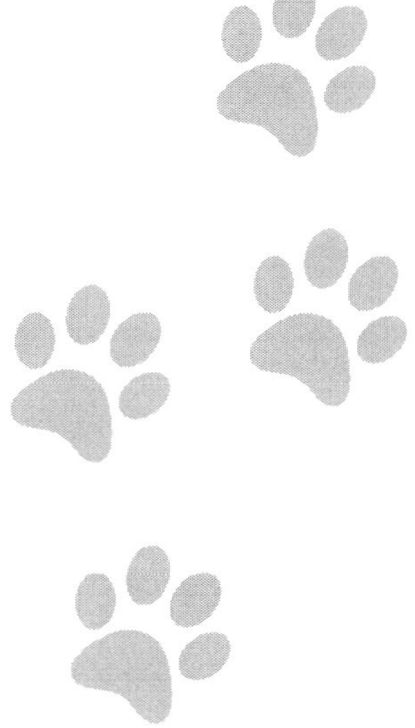

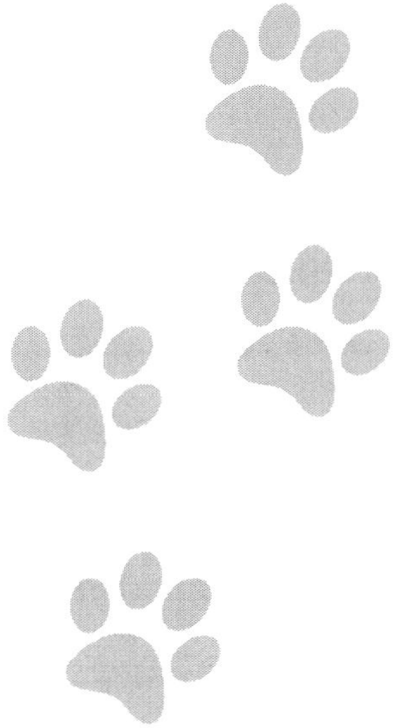

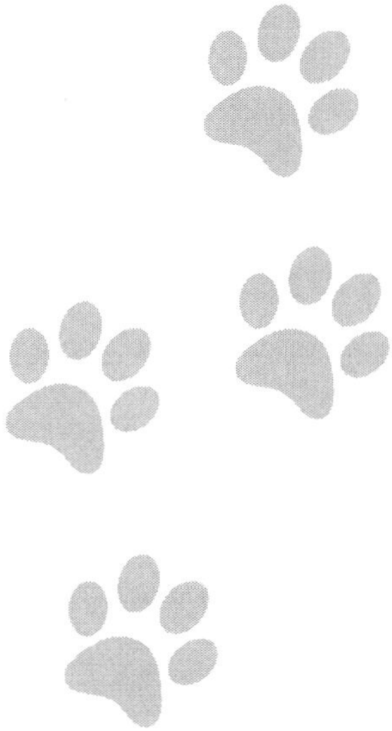

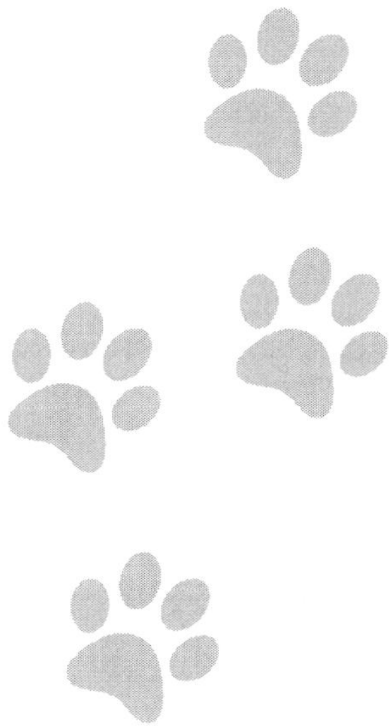

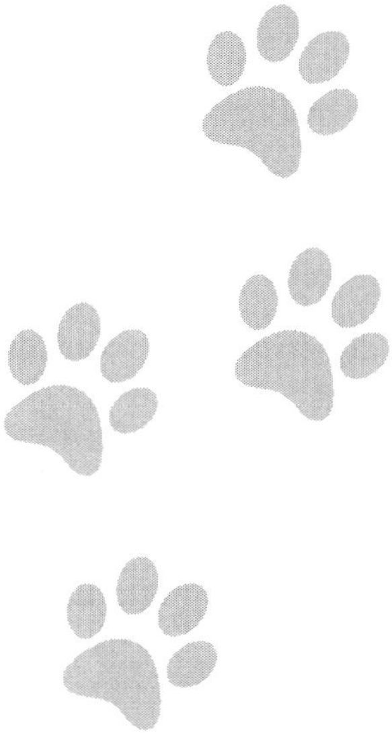

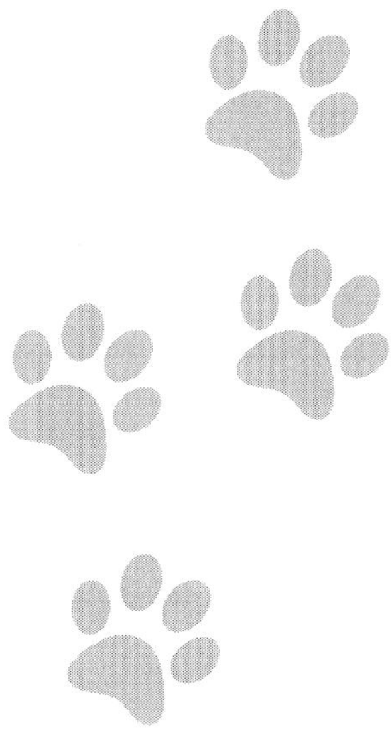

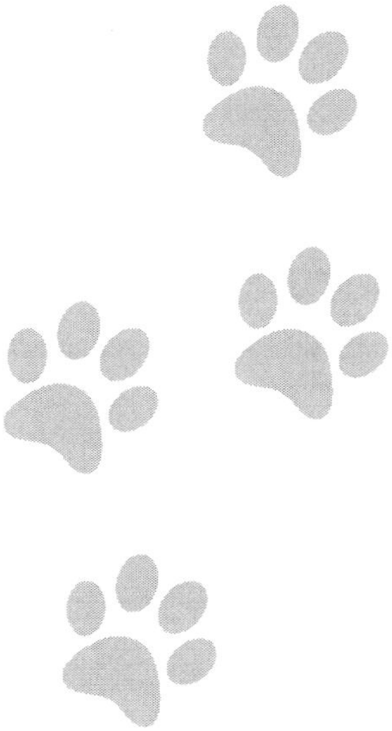

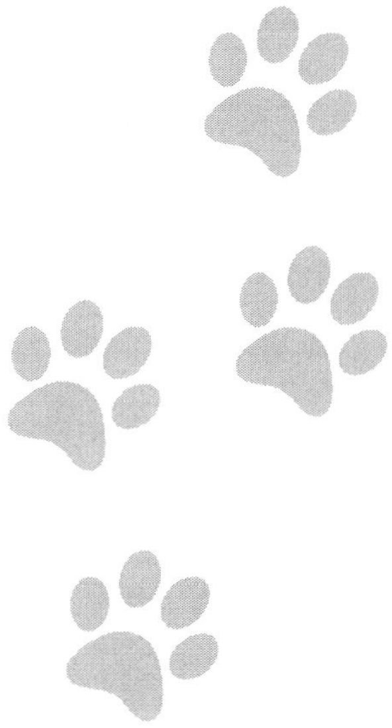

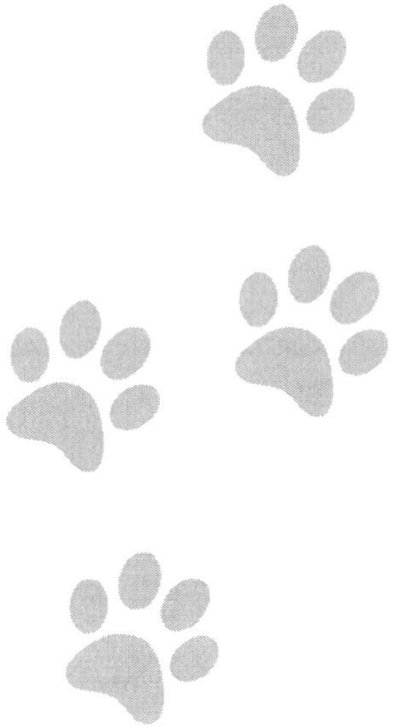

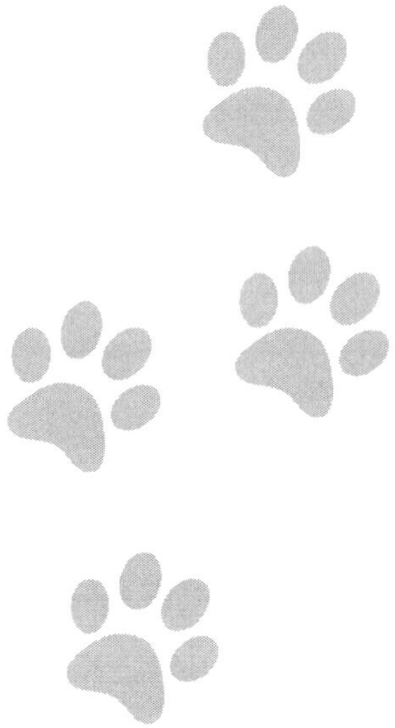

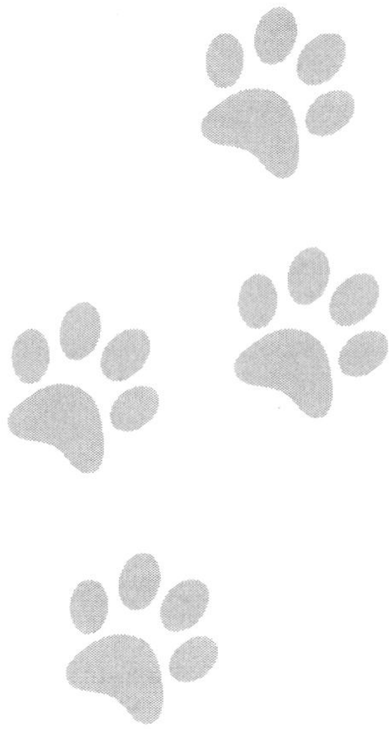

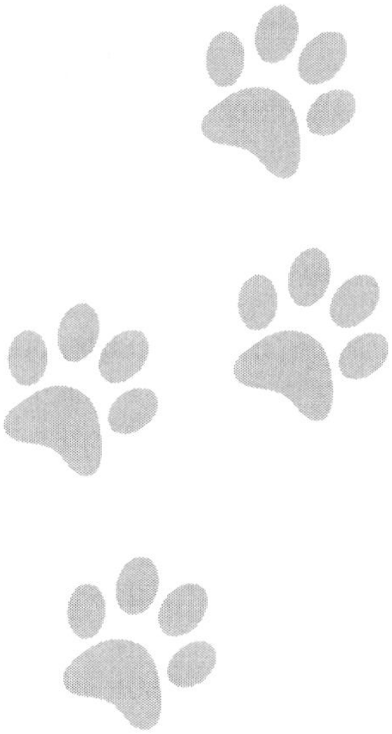

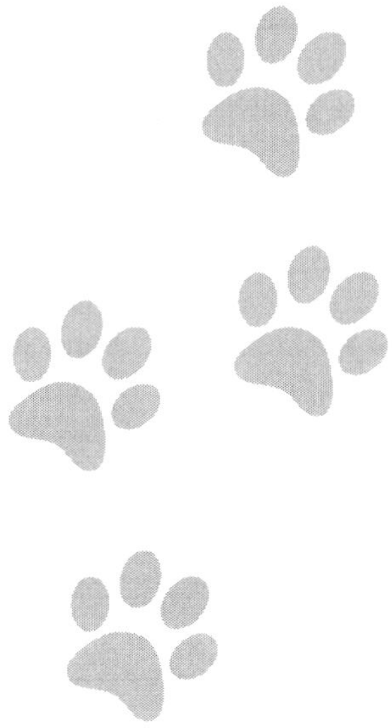

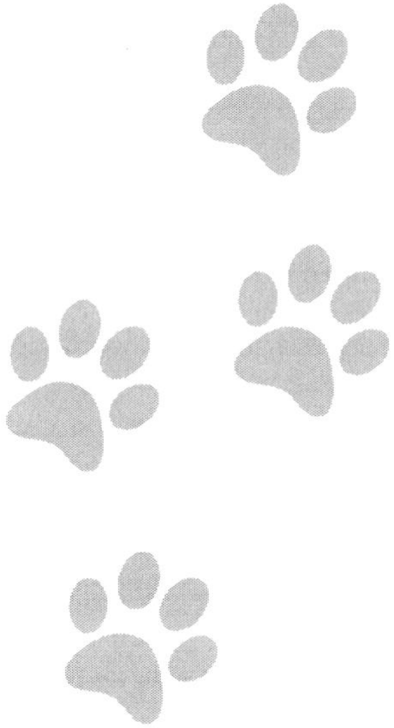

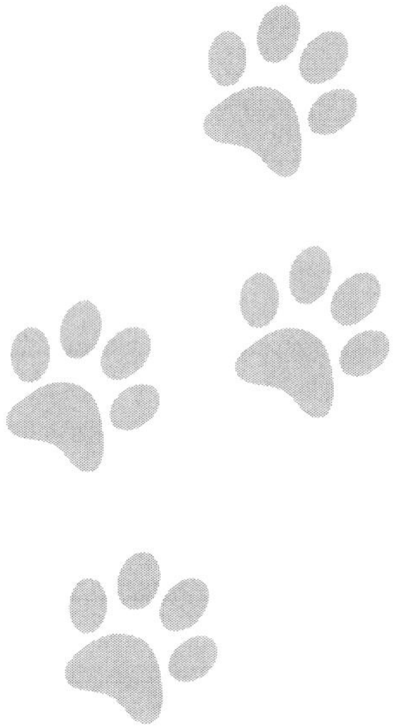

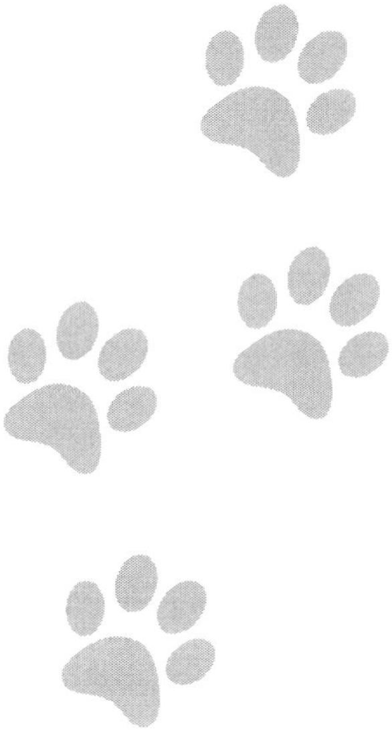

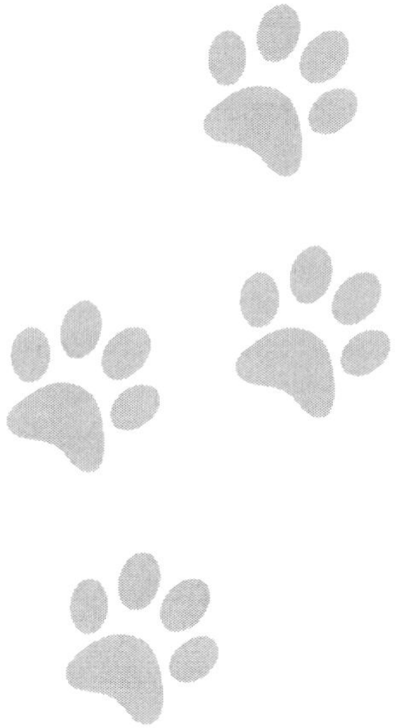

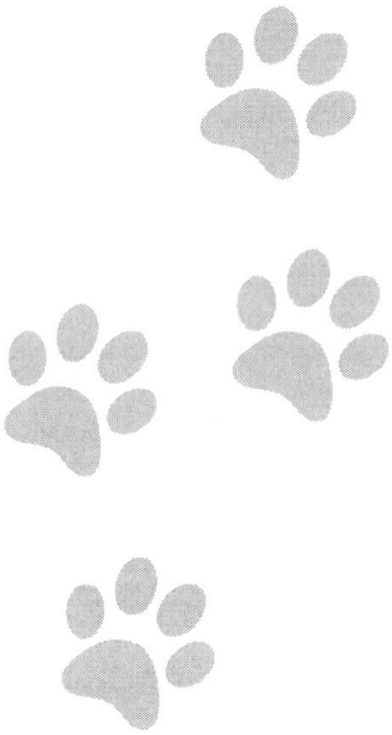

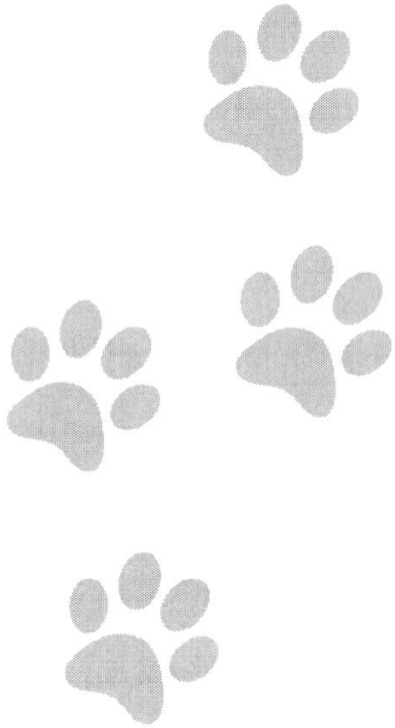

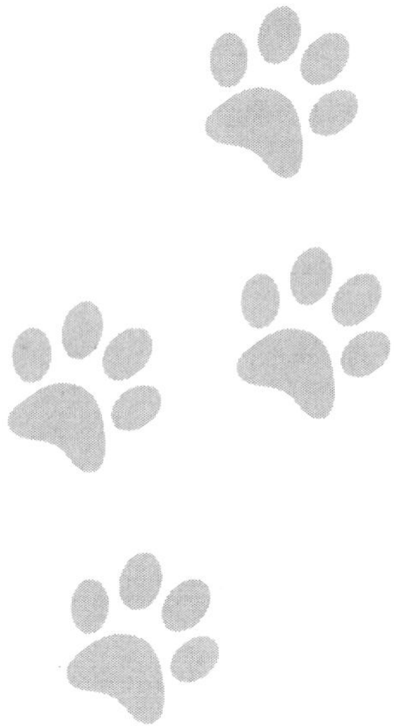

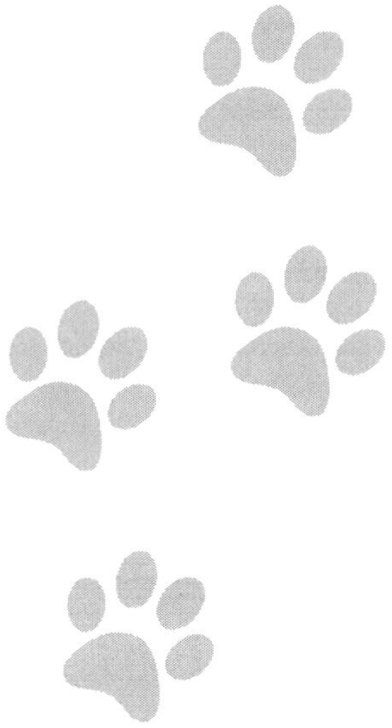

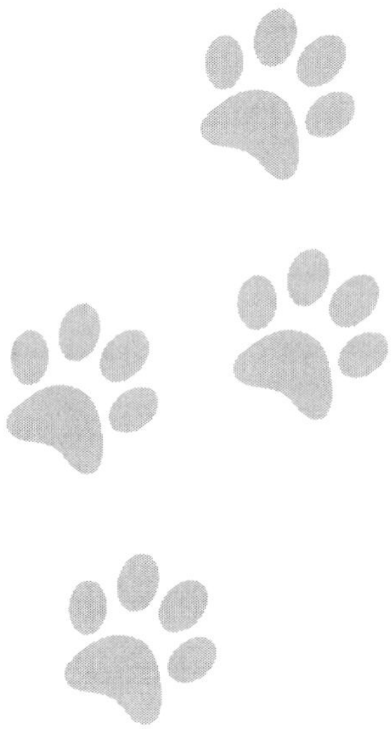

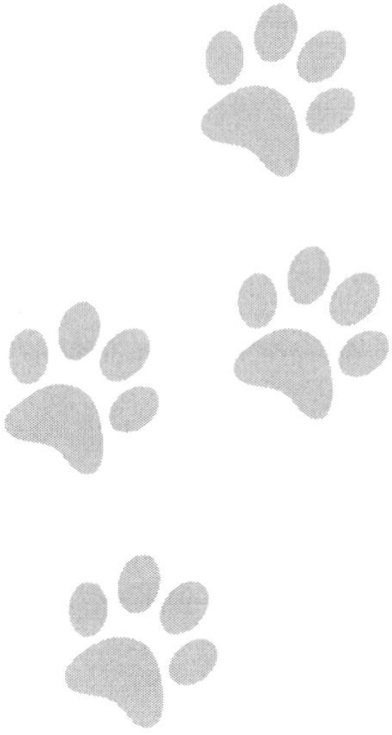

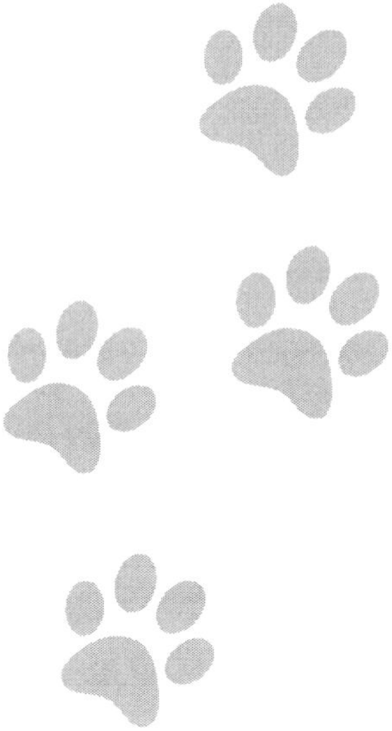

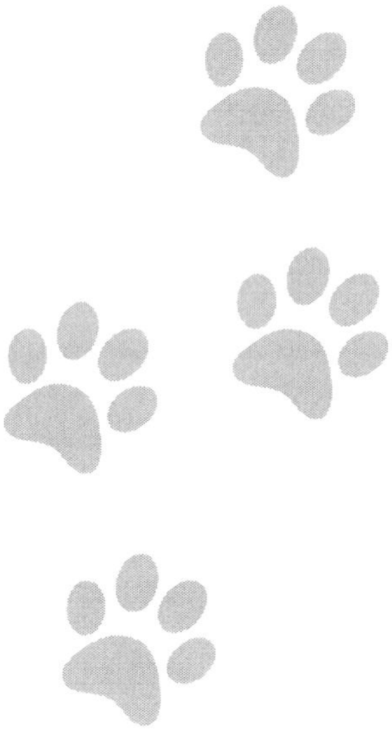

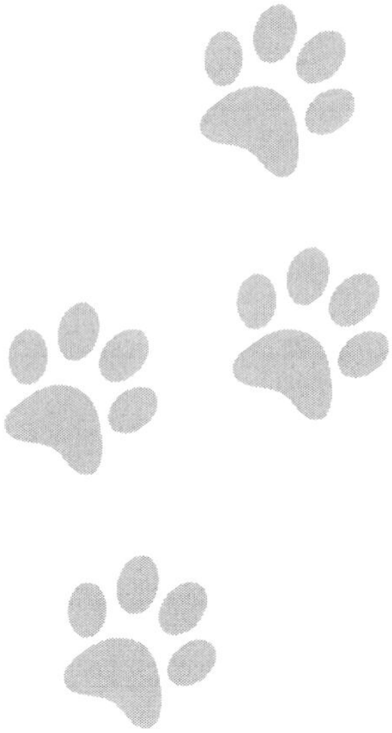

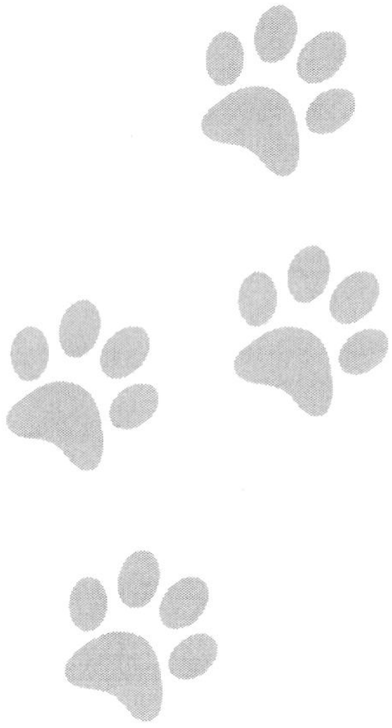

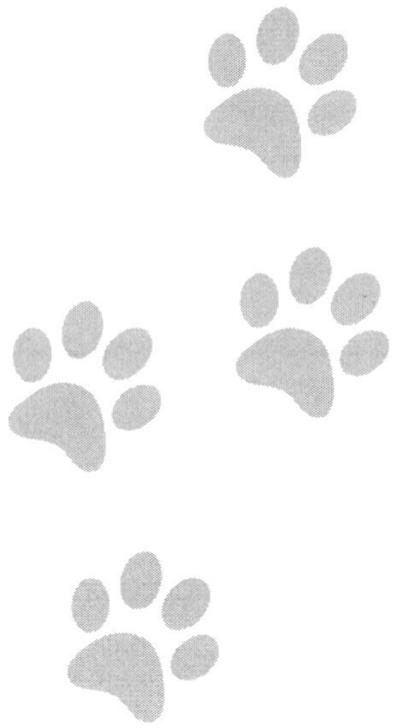

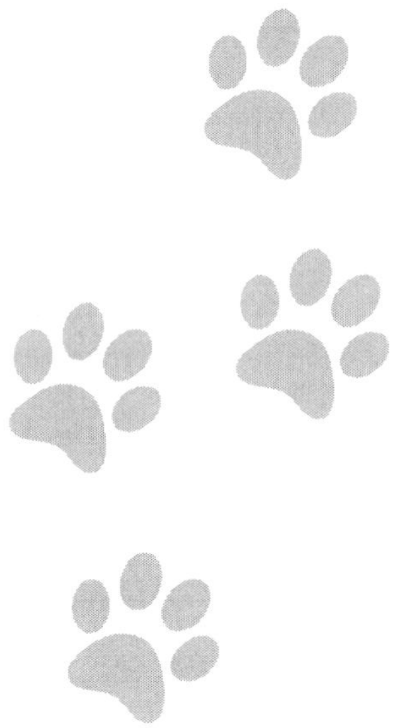

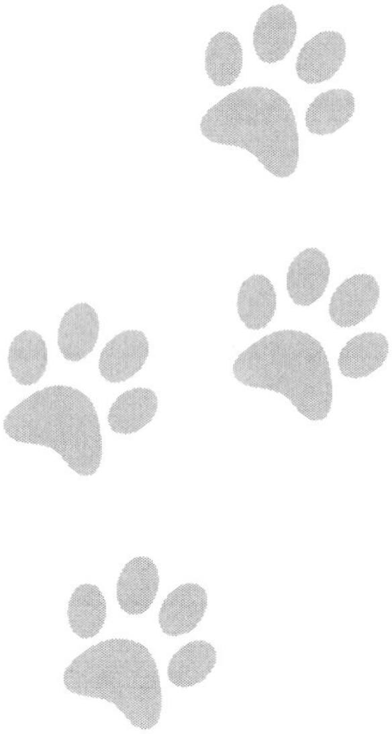